OBSERVING NATURE

Seagull

Written by Stephen Savage

Illustrated by André Boos

Wayland

Ant   Blackbird

Butterfly   Duck

Frog   Oak tree

Rabbit   Salmon

Seagull   Spider

Series editor: Francesca Motisi
Designer: Jean Wheeler

First published in 1995 by
Wayland (Publishers) Ltd
61 Western Road, Hove
East Sussex BN3 1JD, England

British Library Cataloguing in Publication Data
Savage, Stephen
Seagull.- (Observing Nature Series)
I. Title II. Boos. André III Series
598.338

ISBN 0-7502-1522-4

Printed and bound in Italy by
G. Canale & C.S.p.A., Turin
Typeset by Jean Wheeler

Contents

What is a gull?

When you visit the seashore, you are almost certain to see seagulls. There are several large sea birds that we call seagulls, the type you see most often is the herring gull.

Herring gulls have large wings that are good for gliding above the waves. They also have waterproof feathers and webbed feet for swimming.

Male and female

Unlike blackbirds and mallard ducks, the male and female herring gull look the same. Both male and female gulls make the noisy 'owww-owww-owww' call that you often hear.

Although herring gulls are common at the seaside,
they can also be seen at rubbish tips and on farmland.
You may see herring gulls flying in a
V-shaped pattern. They will be either flying to
the coast to feed, or to their roost to rest.

Flocks

For most of the year herring gulls live in large noisy groups called flocks. They often follow fishing boats in the hope of finding some scraps of fish.

Herring gulls can pick up
food from the surface
of the sea with their
beaks. They are not
fussy whether the
food is dead or
alive. They never
miss the chance
to beg for food from
holiday-makers. They
will even eat food that
has been dropped, such as
bread, chips or even pizza.

9

Cracking a shell

Herring gulls have a special way of catching food such as mussels. The herring gull picks the mussel up in its beak and flies high into the sky. Then the gull opens its beak and drops the mussel until the shell is broken.

Herring gulls sometimes eat other birds' eggs and chicks. They will eat dead sea creatures and look for food on rubbish tips. Because they can eat almost anything, herring gulls are able to live almost anywhere.

Making a nest

Herring gulls prefer to nest high up on a cliff. The male and female build the nest together. The nest is rather untidy and is made of grasses, seaweed and other bits and pieces that they find.

Some herring gulls choose to nest on the roof-tops of houses in seaside towns. Human visitors are not so happy about being woken up early in the morning by their noisy calls.

Laying the eggs

In the early summer, the female lays three eggs. However, the eggs are not all laid on the same day. The female gull will only lay one egg each day. Both the female and male take it in turn to sit on the eggs.

Apart from keeping the eggs warm, the herring gulls must keep an eye out for danger. After three and a half weeks, the first egg is ready to hatch.

The eggs hatch

The first chick pecks its way out of the egg. The chick is wet and tired after hatching and needs to rest. As it rests, the chick's downy feathers become dry and fluffy. The second chick hatches two days later. After another two days, the last chick has hatched.

Like all baby birds, the herring gull chicks are always hungry. The parent birds now have the difficult job of feeding their chicks.

Feeding the chicks

The chicks are fed by both parents. They catch fish at
sea, which they bring back for the chicks. This food is
carried in the adult gull's crop which is in its throat.

The adult gulls have a red spot on their beaks.

The chicks must peck at this spot before the adult

gull will feed them.

Dangers

The nest is not very
well hidden and the chicks
are in danger of being attacked and
eaten. When the chicks are only one week old they
leave the nest and hide nearby. The chicks' brown
feathers help them hide.

When an adult herring gull returns to the nest it makes a special call. When the chicks hear this call, they come out of hiding to be fed. The biggest danger comes from black-backed gulls and other large sea birds.

Learning to fly

Over the next five weeks the chicks become bigger and stronger. They flap their wings and hop about, soon they will be ready to fly. Suddenly, the first young gull opens its wings to the wind and flies for the first time. It is quickly followed by its brothers and sisters.

The male and female herring gulls may continue to feed the young gulls for a few days. However, they are now old enough to look after themselves.

Young gulls

Although the young herring gulls are as big as their parents, they still have brown feathers. The three young herring gulls soon join up with other young herring gulls.

They quickly learn to catch food and keep an
eye out for scraps dropped by holiday-makers.
On a calm day, they rest together on the sea,
bobbing up and down with the waves.

Growing up

The young gulls are now two years old, but they still have some brown feathers. Although they are not yet adults, they are just as noisy as their parents.

It will be another three years before the young gulls are the same colour as their parents. Then they will be ready to mate, build a nest and have young of their own.

Other gulls

Here are three other types of gull that you may see. The black-headed gull is smaller than the herring gull and has a dark almost black head. In the winter it only has a black mark above its eyes.

black-headed gull

lesser
black-backed gull

great black-backed gull

The great black-backed
gull is the largest of the
three gulls and has a black
back and wings. The lesser
black-backed gull is about
the size of the herring gull.

Life cycle of a gull

1 Male and female

2 Flocks

3 Cracking a shell

4 Making a nest

5 Laying the eggs

6 The eggs hatch

7 Feeding the chicks

8 Dangers

9 Learning to fly

10 Young gulls

11 Growing up

Glossary

crop A pouch-like part of a bird's throat where food is stored.

gliding Flying easily and smoothly, without the gull having to flap its wings.

roost A place like a perch or a branch, where birds rest or sleep.

waterproof Does not let water in.

webbed Toes connected by a thin fold of skin.

Index